the synesthete's rainbow

the synesthete's rainbow

poetry in the colors of love

NISHA SRINIVASA

SHE WRITES PRESS

Copyright © 2026 Nisha Srinivasa

All rights reserved. No part of this publication may be reproduced, stored in a retrieval system, or transmitted in any form or by any means, electronic, mechanical, photocopying, recording, or otherwise, except for brief quotations in reviews, educational works, or other uses permitted by copyright law.

Published in 2026 by
She Writes Press, an imprint of The Stable Book Group

32 Court Street, Suite 2109
Brooklyn, NY 11201
https://shewritespress.com
Library of Congress Control Number: 2026931299
ISBN: 979-8-89636-128-2
eISBN: 979-8-89636-129-9

Interior Designer: Tabitha Lahr

Printed in the United States

Names and identifying characteristics have been changed to protect the privacy of certain individuals.

No part of this publication may be used to train generative artificial intelligence (AI) models. The publisher and author reserve all rights related to the use of this content in machine learning.

All company and product names mentioned in this book may be trademarks or registered trademarks of their respective owners. They are used for identification purposes only and do not imply endorsement or affiliation.

Dedicated to the ones that have made me experience life in rich, vivid color, for better or for worse. Because of you, my life has transformed into a smattering of rainbow that will eventually turn into healing.

Thank you to my family and my friends for believing in me even when I don't believe in myself.

curving upward

rainbow (beginning)

You lead me down a wayward road untraveled
with your sparkling eyes
and half-done hairdo.

I don't know who you are
but I immediately want to find out.

My quest for
a pot of gold
is starting with you.

(sunrise) yellow

I catch a glimpse of you on the horizon
and as you peak through to say hello
I stand in awe.
I've never seen anything so beautiful.

walnut

You were notoriously a tough one to crack
but I guess I have the right tools
because you tell me things
that no one's ever learned about you.
It's almost like you were waiting for me
to set you free.

eggshell

You pick me up with your fingertips,
examine me as the mystery I remain in your eyes,
and exclaim that I'm light as a feather
before gently tapping me
and coaxing me out.

For others it takes time
but for you I burst open
immediately.

No one else has quite known how to handle me.

plaid

I tell you I can hear patterns
and think to myself
I'll never hear from you again.
"I know that's weird,"
I say while squinting my eyes.
Instead, you pick my brain,
kiss my lips,
and whisper
Tell me more.

We're a perfect crossover—
unexpected, but perfect—
and I love being weird because of you.

mahogany

The floorboards creak below us
as we sit on the floor.
A bottle of wine is the only furniture you have;
we bought it together.
But I sip on your smile
and gorge myself in your hair and your skin
as you graze my fingertips.

We drunkenly dance to
a wedding song,
sloppily stumbling over each other's feet.
You're leading us
and I happily follow;
I always follow you.

As you hold me in your arms,
I let myself submit to my own mind
for the first time.

Maybe this really could be something.

white (light)

My dreams are a dark place,
so I never let myself visit.
Even when you run your silky fingers through my
mop of hair,
finding your way from one strand to the next,
it's hard to fathom that someone like you
could ever love me.

But you take my hand and lead me there,
to the place I never let myself visit,
my dreams,
and with you here
I let myself dream in a way that I never have before—
toward a world in which we
are ours.

pink

The lights in my room shine when you walk in,
cascading over you, as if to say
you're mine.
My heart beats a million times
when you finally kiss me;
dopamine puts on its ballet slippers,
leaping across every axon in my brain,
and my cheeks become neon wisps of cotton candy
melting into you.

I guess I'm yours too.

cyan (lightning)

My brain hasn't known
a color like that of your love.
It's explosive,
electric.
All I can do is smile
as your wondrous bolt
flashes before my eyes.

purple (silk)

I'm a tangled web of
family secrets,
self-doubt,
and excess
unwanted.

But you manage to
see through my impenetrable knots.

blue (bubbles)

Hours of talking
feel like minutes of whispering.
With you I can always be louder,
say more,
and speak my mind.

aquamarine

We dip our toes in the water
and play mermaids like we've known each other
for years.
Everything feels easy with you.

Like holding my breath underwater,
being with you
is instinctive,
natural.

When we dive underneath the waves
and tumble around in the undertow,
I know you're the person I love.

red (bursts)

We invented
the snap, crackle, and pop of the fireworks
that grace a clear summer sky.
My heart bursts into bits of sparkle
every time you utter my name.

peach(y keen)

You wrap your arms around me
and I reverb to the touch of your love
before settling into you.

amaranth

You're my sustenance.
It feels like the more of you I get
the more of me I become.

cerulean

I didn't believe in love at first sight
until I discovered cerulean in
a box of crayons.

It called to me
just like you did
the moment I laid eyes on you.

(blush)

I'm swirled in your love
like cotton candy clouds dancing in the air.
My cheeks match my heart in color
as your eyes lift me off the ground.

I've never been this embarrassed—
but I've never been this in love before either.

pink (cheeks)

Your laugh is
my favorite color.

I could listen to it forever.

midnight blue

Like a little girl,
I kick my feet underneath my fort made of bedsheets
any time my phone light shines.
Talking to you all night
is wistful and easy,
and I never want it to end.

peach

X marks the spot that
leads me to you.
I open you up
and discover all your hidden treasures.
My eyes glimmer as I look at your diamonds and pearls
knowing I'd never touch another thing
as precious as what comes from you.

clear

I'm in love with you
and nothing has ever been more certain.

black (box)

I think that I take up too much space,
always tripping and falling off my marks.
But you step aside
to make more room for me
and let me have the spotlight.

white(board)

I'm an empty space
on which you can flood your thoughts.
Whether you write in cursive or in print,
your wildest dreams,
your deepest fears,
your bold ideas,
or what your heart holds near,
I'll always be here
to receive you.

pearl

I hear you
in the same way I hear a love song;
your melody is bright
and soothing.

I could listen to it,
You,
on repeat.

magenta

I know that I'm loud
but somehow you match my volume.
We take on the world,
screaming together as one.

yellow (pages)

I flip through all the
pages of the old book you finally
lent me.
I see your markings, cross-outs,
footnotes
that reveal the inner workings of your mind.
I can smell your words
and taste your brilliance.

I'm already craving
my next You original.

chocolate

I start to melt between your fingers
and
my semi sweet surface
becomes saccharine.

vantablack

Our love is so rare,
it was only just given a name.
It's hard to find
and harder to replicate.

everclear

I know you.
Therefore, I know love.

multicolored

I transform my rosy skies
into violet rays
because you told me you liked how they looked.
But when you ask me to make them blue,
Red,
any shade of green or purple,
hues of yellow or orange,
an amalgamation of
burgundies and cranberries,
pinks and browns,

of course, I say yes.

There's nothing I wouldn't do for you
and I want to be what you want.

I want to be who you want.

lapis (lazuli)

The color of sleep is a gemstone so precious.
But in you
I have a jewel.
I feel awake
and alive
every second I spend with you.

brown

You look at my skin.
You say it's beautiful.
I haven't heard that before
from any other human I loved.

Brown glimmers in your eyes.

emerald

All that glitters is
green
so when you bat your eyelids
I grow weak in the knees.

umber

You call me a work of art;
admiring my warm, earthy tones
against the pallor of you(r canvas).

You'll be famous someday!
you exclaim
as you're the first to make a discovery in me.

mahogany (building)

I lay a foundation
to be the sturdy, brilliant, and sparkling vision
you have of me in your head.
I see bricks, but you see a future—
a person that I could be.
So, for you, I learn the art of construction
and build myself up.

light blue

Whenever I'm with you
the sky looks wispy
like it does in my dreams.
Strokes of light blue
dance through my mind
when I look at you.

So I can only hope that I'm still awake.

crimson

Are you happy?
you ask.

Indescribably so,

I answer.

?

Having synesthesia means that sometimes
I hear colors
that don't exist.
My superpower must apply to relationships too,
because like those colors,
we're hard to describe
to anyone else

but you get it.

Right?

orange (juice)

You tell me,

Squeeze out every drop of me
and pour me into your cup
in the morning.

I know I'm good for you.

(Ignore the nutrition label.)

gold (midas touch)

Everything you touch
turns to gold
in my brain.
Those things, those memories
become permanent,
untouchable.

red (clay)

You run through my mind
every day
without stopping.
I wonder whether you'll get tired at some point.
But you never do.
You keep on going.

gold (dust)

Everyone says your words are starting to sound like hot air.
But that's what stars are made of
and you shine brightly to me.

rose

You shine so brightly
that I need glasses to see you.
So I buy the best rose colored pair on the market
and look at you for hours.
No one else understands
that I see you as perfect.

neon pink

is the color of the toolbox I pull out
whenever you tell me a sad story—
most of the stories you tell me are.

But fear not.
As your personal handywoman,
I'm always ready to fix you
and your problems.

black (ice)

The road ahead seems slippery
but you convince me that it's only smooth
so I keep on.

(pale) blue

I'm starting to crave you
in a way that an animal inching toward a stream
on a hot day
craves water.

I desperately need you to survive.

(hot) blue

I wished on a star
for a love like yours
that streams across the sky,
but as I get closer to you
the more it hurts.

Stars are for dreaming, though.
So I'll keep trying.

silver

I see your face in my mirror,
hear your words in my mouth,
and your laugh in my ears;
grip the strands of your thick wavy hair
between my fingers
and feel my bones ache
for your gaze.

red-orange

I blend into you
and become indiscriminate—
there is no me without you.

red, yellow, blue

I mix my primaries to make you new colors.
But it isn't enough.

I'm running out of combinations,
out of ways to make you happy.

sea foam

I see that your love for me is waning.
It starts to ebb and flow
like the waves that crash on the shore.
For a moment, they come and leave all kinds of treasures,
secrets in the form of seashells,
but eventually they drift away
looking breathtakingly beautiful,
nonetheless.

rose (petals)

You love me,
love me not,
love me,
(. . . or love me not?)

fuchsia

Why do you now hold out your arm
to help me
and start to retract it when I decide
to take it?

purple (noticings)

I smile widely
as you taunt me with your
blistered indifference.

violet

Your excuses are mellifluous,
tickling my eardrums like a beautifully
discordant song;
I only hear the good notes when
everyone around me tells me
how awful it all sounds together
because I can't believe you'd ever tell me
a lie.

blue (stripes)

You expect me
to read in between the lines
even though they're faint,
blurry,
and practically invisible.

multicolored (wheel)

The more you ignore me,
the more I need you
and I spin around in circles
until you reply.

purple (lyre)

You were sent to rescue me
and I beg for you to turn my way,
to sing for me your sweet melodies—
only when you do,
I begin to wither away.

bubblegum pink

When I'm sick
I become dependent on medicine
that fixes the pain
but not the problem.

And still, I continue to take it.

Being with you is my medicine.
I'm dependent on you,
even though you never leave me
feeling healed.

[insert color here]

I don't know what to call this poem
in the same way you don't know what
to call us.

forty-two degrees (below)

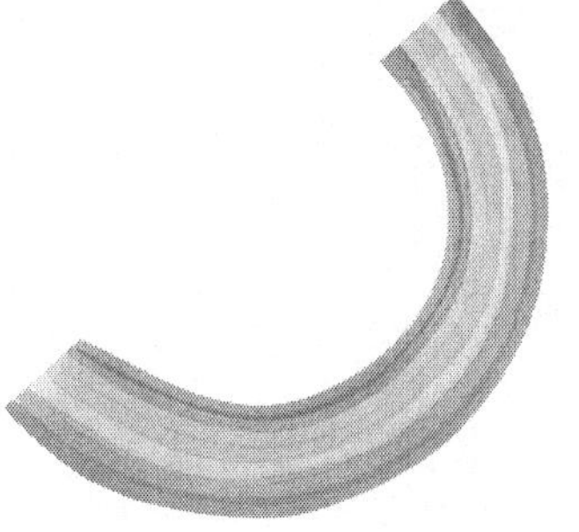

beige

We are explosive,
fiery,
vibrant,
until you decide you want to stop painting with me.

You cover me in a dull quiet
I'd never known from you before.
You put me on the shelf as quickly as
you took me off of it
and watch
as dust accumulates on my surface
fills my lungs
and sweeps me away.

heliotrope

I plant my garden
as if you're the sun
and my flowers beg you
for life.

Please, look at me.

charcoal (part one)

I put myself through fire
and watch myself slowly burn.

As I turn into ash,
I think to myself,

This is worth it
if it makes you happy.

burgundy

You chip away at my
complex layers
unveiling my smooth surface,
leaving me raw,
vulnerable,
exposed,
and decide to paint over me anyway.

cream

I am a work of art
created in your image—
so why do you cover me up
like I mean nothing to you?

gradient

How did you go from saying
love
to *loved*
within a matter of days?

turquoise

The phrase “I’m sorry”
sounds like turquoise in my ears.
Because of you,
I’m accustomed to hearing it all the time.
Your
“I’m sorrys”
are sprinkled with embers of your pain—
pain that justifies the ways in which
you hurt me.

But at least they sound lovely coming from you.
So I don’t mind.

blue

You smile every time you prick my veins,
injecting me with the sharpest of needles,
and watch the blood pour out of me.
I know what you do.
You are calculated,
your methods transparent
and predictable.
Yet, each time I sit down next to you
I give you my arm willingly.

cherry (picking)

I finally take note
of your selection in love.
You love single strands of my hair
but never my entire head,
my irises
but never the tears that fall from them,
my smile
but never my frown.

You love me when I am perfect
but never when I am myself.

brown and white

On a dime,
you hate the color brown
and say you don't even see it anymore.

So do you see me at all?

I promise, I can make myself more palatable to you.

black and white (love)

I thought there were only two options when it came to love:
to be loved
or to not be.
But you break me out of the binary
and show me it's possible
to feign it.

red (light)

Your affection comes to a screeching halt

so of course, I crash.

red (stalemate)

Give me an *x*,
give me an *o*.
I stare you down
in the dreary hope that I can still win over you
(win you over).

We're both either too good
or equally bad
at playing the game
and now we're stuck.

No one wins.

brown (dirt)

You say you're
an environmentalist.
But now that you're done with me,
you crumple me up
and casually throw me on the ground,
littering your carelessness
and oblivion
for someone else in my life
to pick up.

gray

To you, I guess I was always
I could
but never *I will,*
and I got comfortable
nestling in between your
complex emotions
while ignoring my own.

purple (silk) edited

I'm a tangled web of
family secrets,
self-doubt,
and excess
unwanted.

But you manage to . . .
~~see through my impenetrable knots.~~

add knots to my constricted form
as you tie me to your brain
and tether me to your thoughts.

indigo

The color most often forgotten in the rainbow—
clandestinely vibrant,
seen, yet never remembered.

Guess it makes sense that this was
your nickname for me.

(burnt) orange

You impose a tariff on me,
cut me off from my resources,
starve me,
and let me bleed out.

And still, you expect me to survive.

golden (burning)

For you I touch the sun
with my bare hands
only to be burned more
by your silence.

gray (area)

I hate you until you say my name—
the very moment you remind me that
I'm in a purgatory
of loveless love.

white

So what happens now?
I don't know where to go from here.

mazarine

You only use it
when you paint for me—
and yet, you call me a
“dear friend.”

yellow (bellied)

I watch another version of me
stand up for myself
and demand that you treat me better
while I silently submit to your
cowardice.

puce

I settle so deeply into you
that I lose sight of myself.
I gasp for air
as I fight for space in between
the crevices of your grip.

black(out)

Your flip of a switch
turns my lights off
for what seems like forever.

leopard print

People confuse leopards and cheetahs
in the same way I confused your compliments
for love.
To you, they meant nothing more
than friendship
but I'm still covered in spots
that mark where you kissed me.

black(board)

You try to wipe our memories away
with a chalky foam eraser.
But the remnants of my cursive, cursed love
are scattered all over my worn down
surface.

purple

You're like a powerful sorceress
with dark fingernails
and a jubilant, yet menacing laugh;
telepathy is your power.
You always find a way to enter my mind.

I'm the heroine who screams
with all her might
for you to be gone,
for you to free me
from the torment of you.

(hunter) green

My brain always used to expect the worst
and hope for the best
until you came along
and rewired it.
Now, I expect the best
and get crushed
when I realize
that you continue to give me your worst.

silver (platter)

You act as if
I didn't serve you
my entire
Heart
and
Soul
and you still remain
starved of decision.

black

I said I'd never get a tattoo
but you gave me one I didn't ask for;
a seemingly indelible mark
that made me believe that one day,
I could be loved by you.
But it's because of you that I'm learning
just how bitterly painful it is
to remove tattoos—
the ones you didn't realize you wanted
but so desperately did
in actuality.

It's possible.
But damn, does it hurt.

gray(ness, insecurity)

With a swathe of your finest gray paints,
you made me go from asking *When I will be loved?*
to wondering if I'll be loved at all.

copper

I was your conductor,
letting your wild energy run through me
as I was bent,
twisted,
and reshaped.

green

It's my least favorite color,
that is, until I meet you
and you paint my whole world in its
emerald, forest, and lime hues.
I think that my life, like the earth, will be healthier,
happier
with more green in it,
with more of you in it.

But I forget that green is also synonymous with
greed.

From me, you take everything.

gold (thief)

You rob me of being loved
by both you
and myself.

red (bloodshed)

I stitch my gaping wound that you left
with a thread so thick
scissors consider it an
arch nemesis.
I watch as the frayed fibers of my skin
fuse together
after spending years of being
brutally carved apart.

Through the pain, I inhale
the lies you fed to me
and exhale closure.
And yet somehow you unravel my hard work
with a single pull
that is painless and effortless.
Willingly, I'll crawl back to you
while internally begging for relief
knowing that I have to
start healing
all over again.

scarlet

Sick
with love,
lovesick,
sick from loving you,
sick of loving you—
I don't even know
when the fever started,
but I've been burning up,
hopelessly lost
without a cure
in sight.

red (with envy)

I screamn
WHY DON'T YOU LOVE ME?
without ever uttering a word,
and become jealous of you
because I realize that
you experienced a love
I've never received,
but so desperately want.

maroon

Why is it that you would fight in an instant about me,
but never for me?

black (hole)

I absorbed your rays of sunshine,
grief,
pain,
love,
confusion,
and denial
only to be left with darkness in the end.

red (in the face)

From Marathon to Athens,
I ran
but you won't meet me halfway.
I crawl to the finish line
on my hands and knees
begging for your love.

green (vine)

Why am I holding on to you
when you've already left me?

red (track)

I'm still stuck at the 200-meter mark,
the place where we nearly turned the corner together,
but you sped ahead
and finished the race,
leaving me in the dust.

yellow-neutral

You tell me I need to tone myself down,
become neutral,
even though my undertone is the warmest of warm.
For you I buy a coverup,
a concealer
that doesn't match me at all
so that you'll see me as the one you want.
But with a furious swipe of remover
you take away what protects me from
the gaze of your piercingly gentle eyes.

As you look at my blemishes
I realize that
It,
Her,
the one you love
is never going to be me.

green (line, lie)

I laugh when you tell me
that you'll take the other train to our final destination
before I realize that you're headed in the opposite direction,
never intending to meet me where I'm going.

yellow (wood)

We diverged long before
we got to the path.

(faded) rose

You love me not.

(sterling) silver

Was any of it real to you?

burnt sienna

I reach for you one last time
before

tripping,

falling,

failing.

crimson (drain)

Are you happy?
you ask again.

Indescribably so,

I lie.

the pot of gold, recovery

white (flag)

I surrender.

beige (quilt)

I try to put myself together again
but I exist in patches—
my stitching visible
and my heart exposed
to the caprice of anyone who decides to use me.

black (top)

I learn to enjoy the ground
where you left me lying in pain
and I start finding comfort
in the fact that
it can't get any worse than this.

baby, pink

Somehow,
after all that,
I'll never forget what you wore
on the day we met.

It's my favorite color, after all.

chocolate (surprise)

I guess it was bittersweet after all.

yellow (noon)

Time stopped with you
and now that you're gone,
the clock has started to move—

but I'm stuck in the seconds just before.

lilac

It is taking me too long to let you go,
because losing you
is losing a part of me
that felt beautiful
and seen,
the part of me that convinced myself that love
never belonged to me in the first place
so I'm lucky to at least have had a taste.

indigo (to) violet

I thought I saw your shadow
around the corner.
It wasn't you
but it had your controlled smile,
thick nails,
and echoing laughter
and in that moment,
I became ready to fall in lust again.

ice blue

I now freeze whenever you come to mind—
bitter cold runs through my veins
and rushes toward my heart
as I think of what you did to me.

(pitch) black

Because of you,
I only love so much.
It is a verb so calculated
and pre-determined,
cautiously given in doses.

After knowing you,
I'll never give it freely.

gray (matter)

For years,
I thought it was my fault.

But then I grew up.

And with my now fully developed brain
I can confidently declare
that it was yours.

navy

I'm the sun.
But instead of letting my rays shine,
I gravitate toward forces that dim my light.
It's why I loved you.
I lied in between your sheets
and you smiled as you took in my glow,
became sun-kissed
as I made you feel special.
I made you brighter.

orange

Just like the leaves,
I saw the real you only for a short while
before you decomposed
and disappeared,
before you forgot about me.
But all I can think about
is how magnificently beautiful you were
on those cool autumn days.

orange (love)

When you were bitter,
no one loved you but me—
but now that you've acquired an
artificial sweetness,
I'm sure you're more palatable
to someone who wants to
rot their teeth in your
acidic promises.

blue(print)

I'm an architect
who designs perfect versions of myself.
They'd call me a marvel
and you'd sport a smile carved by world class carpenters
as you tore up my plans,
the versions of me I worked so hard
to map out
for you.

But even though you ruined my blueprints,
you could never take my tools.
Compass, protractor, and confidence in hand,
I begin another sketch of a life I'll lead for myself
and myself only.

charcoal (part two)

From the ashes,
Christ was born,
phoenixes rose,
and souls went to heaven.
All myths alike have
a reprise,
a renewal.

You burned me.
So I know that one day
I'll rise from my own
ruin.

red (yearning)

They say that home is where the heart is.
I wonder if that also applies to broken hearts
because if that's the case,
you'll always be home to me.

gray (shadows)

And we can never be friends

because my life gets temporarily derailed
whenever you decide to remember
that I exist.

black and white (messages)

teal

Every kind word I said to you was
dripping with sincerity.
My integrity is a greater gift
than your excuse for love
ever could be.

plaid (repeating)

Finally,
after years of back and forth,
I broke the pattern.

black and white (letter)

I write to you with a fervor
I possess not in speaking.
On paper I am angry.
But by tongue my anger vanquishes
and becomes everlasting patience.

sand

Even if you weren't meant to be mine,
I'm glad I got to know myself in love
and affirm that in the vast expanse of my heart
I'll eventually be able to make room for another.

jade

You throw me
headfirst
into the Pactolus
and I think my fate is sealed.

Instead, instinct kicks in—
one foot after the other—
and I swim my way to the top

Cleansed
and
Free
from your curse.

black (shoes)

We were the same size in shoes,
and I happily let your feet sink into my worn out loafers
when you wanted to borrow them.
But eventually, my feet grew longer,
thicker,
wiser,
as I outgrew you.

olive (branch)

You took my peace,
and though that day is not today,
one day, I'll forgive you for it.

gray-black-yellow

Much like an elephant,
I'll forgive
but I will never forget.

earthy

You're like the weeds in my garden
that block my gorgeous roses from blossoming
and becoming their full selves.
But weeds can always be cut.
I've been snipping away
and finally feel myself
growing.

(pure) gold

With the power of my ancestors,
I'll shine my light
on those that deserve me.

lavender

I still see you
with frill socks
and painted hands
even though you chopped off your hair,
wear dark corduroys,
and use pencils over pens.
You're no longer the person of our youth.
But sometimes when you laugh
I hear your voice from years ago
and I smile knowing that
we're different people now
and that's okay.

blue (jeans)

Like my favorite pair of jeans,
my memories of you are fading over time.

I hate wearing pants anyway.

silver (regent)

I gave up my power
in exchange for your love.

So when I finally realized
I'd never have it,
I reassumed the throne.

I'm ready to rule my own life again.

rosy (compassion)

You weren't ready to receive my love,
but finally,
I am.

(sunset) yellow

I catch a glimpse of you on the horizon
and as you descend
I know that I'll never see you again.
I cry with a smile
knowing that finally,
I can move on.

sunrise yellow

The love of my life is on the horizon.
I can't see them clearly from here
but I know one thing for certain—

it's not you.

indigo (memory)

I think I forgot to remember you.

Is this what breathing actually feels like?

celadon

Still

wherever you are,
I hope you're okay.

I will be, too.

crimson (rest)

Are you happy?
I ask myself for the first time.

Indescribably so,

I say with a refreshed sigh
to signal my gratitude.

It's finally over.

white (winged)

Now I fly with the freedom of a dove
who's just realized
she has wings.

rainbow (the other side)

It took me years
to get here.

I never thought I'd see the end of a rainbow—
because of you
I thought I was meant to live inside one.

But on this side
your voice is muffled
the air doesn't smell like your perfume
and the way you "loved" me is
a thing of the past.

There's no pot of gold.
There's something better.

My freedom.

moonlight blue

But sometimes,
when I look into the night sky
I think of what we could've been.

about the author

NISHA SRINIVASA is a writer, educator, and lover of the arts. Writing has always been her medium of self-expression, a way to explore and articulate the complexities of love, identity, and transformation. Beyond her own creative work, she is passionate about helping others—especially her students—find and share their voices through writing. She earned her bachelor's degree in French and linguistics from UC Berkeley before pursuing her master's at the Harvard Graduate School of Education, where she specialized in human development. Nisha currently resides in Oakland, California.

Author photo © Taylor Nitta

Looking for your next great read?

We can help!

Visit www.shewritespress.com/next-read
or scan the QR code below for a list
of our recommended titles.

She Writes Press is an award-winning
independent publishing company founded to
serve women writers everywhere.